glitter BLESSED

ALREADY WHOLE, ALREADY HOLY

SEAN NEIL-BARRON, EDITOR

ISBN: 979-8-9859137-0-5 (Print)
ISBN: 979-8-9859137-1-2 (Ebook)

Library of Congress Control Number: 2025924066

Any references to historical events, real people, or real places are used fictitiously. Names, characters, and places are products of the author's imagination.

Front cover image by Xan Owens.
Book design by Vivien Reis.

First printing edition 2025.

Foothills Unitarian Church
1815 Yorktown Ave
Fort Collins, Colorado, 80524

foothillsuu.org

For family in all its forms— given, chosen, fought for, found.

For ancestors who carried us here through silence,
through loss, through love that outlasted death.

For those who radicalized me in the ancient,
dangerous art of loving without apology.

For Foothills Unitarian Church, colleagues &
congregents, people willing to trade comfort
for courage, while never forgetting joy.

For every writer who offered blessings that stick &
shimmer directly in the places truth needs to blossom.

For you, holding these words,
continuing what we could only begin.

May you never forget: you are already whole, already holy.

May you know in your bones—this life was always
supposed to feel this tender, this fierce, this yours.

Contents

Introduction

Silence = Death.

Our ancestors knew this when they painted it on signs during the AIDS crisis, when ACT UP understood what we must never forget: silence is contagious, but so is courage.

Breaking that silence is a collective act. We speak and bless each other into being, gifting words to describe these queer existences of ours, stubborn offerings of truth held up on the altars of a life the world keeps insisting we don't get to have.

This collection of blessings was born from that practice. Our hope is that they don't all speak to you, because they're written to speak into the queer uniqueness of our lives.

We've organized these blessings by the
    moments that call for them:

For the Morning, when you need to remember who
    you are before the world tells you otherwise.
For the Breaking Points, when everything
    feels too heavy to carry alone.
For the Celebrations, when joy demands
    witnesses and pride needs proclamation.
For the Quiet Moments, when tenderness is everything.
For the Fight, when resistance is the only
    prayer that makes sense.
For the Future, when we need to conjure
    what we're building together.

Scan the table of contents like a treasure map, where X marks the spot of whatever your heart needs most: courage for the scared, defiance for the defeated, tenderness for the wounded, celebration for the places shame still lives.

GlitterBlessed, the name of this collection, comes from offering Glitter Blessings at Pride. It's a rather simple practice, where you anoint someone with some biodegradable glitter and offer them a blessing.

It's a practice I didn't invent but one that has transformed me. Each blessing I give is unique but I often include the words "You are stardust, made of the same stuff as the stars and the trees and the mountains and rivers, which means you belong here. And there is nothing you can do, nothing you need to do, that can change that."

I hope that this collection brings you the blessing you need, even just for this moment.

Sean Neil-Barron, Editor

FOR THE MORNING

When you need to remember who you are before the world tells you otherwise

This Body is a Holy Place of Change

Silen Wellington

This body is a holy place of change.
Blessed be the worn skin and callous
the memories of monkey bars
and guitar strings on my finger pads
the jump rope,
the cracked knuckles
from dry winters.

Blessed be the place my hand met the asphalt —
Trying to scooter with bright yellow Crocs
the smell of watermelon and grass in the air
as I barreled over the handlebars
Scooter clanging on the ground,
Hands catching my 11-year old body.

Blessed be the cells of my resilient hand,
growing over that scratch
like lattice work
like webs
to grow, grow
heal, heal
Regenerate.

Blessed be that black speck of dirt
reminding me the tightrope between
childhood fun and childhood injury
So easily endured,

learning little by little —
Sometimes the world hurts you.
This body is a holy place of change.

Blessed be the eye crinkle from so many years of joy
The crow's talons that haunt my gaze.

Blessed be the scar where my head split open
the cowlick, the places my hair
grows the wrong way.
Blessed be every cut that healed.

Blessed be the way age softens me,
the smooth lines of scars
becoming less textured
like river currents
making smooth
the stone.

This body is a holy place of change.

Blessed be my eyes
that knew
that saw in the mirror
something Else humming with Life
something Other that made me more alive,
that saw in the mirror
something the spirits wanted to draw forth.

A Truth so ineffable
it could only be followed by faith.

A Truth that sung —
This body needs to shapeshift.

Blessed be the friends that made ritual
        of their testosterone,
that said *Yes, explore this living Myth in your body.*
Trepidatious though we were,
blessed be that we listened anyway.

Blessed be the cartilage that hardened,
that drew my voice lower,
that gave me big enough reeds so
my soul could hum through.

Blessed be the hardened jawline,
the knife's edge that knew when to let go,
to move on, to find those
who would see me for me,
who would honor this
Body that changes.

Blessed be the chin hairs
like adolescent lion scruff.
Blessed be that trans person who taught me
even if everyone else thinks it's a weird neck beard
doesn't make the euphoria any less genuine.

Blessed be the gender euphoria.
the gender clumsy
the gender fails
the gender resurrecting

the gender dreaming
the gender re-imagining
the gender-full.

Blessed be the crescent moon scars on my chest,
The constellation of surgery incisions
shining like bone white stars.

The way I can take a full breath now
the way I can relax my shoulders.
Blessed being this coming home to my body.

Blessed be this body that is an expression of Holy Change.
Come, won't you bless yourself too?
And all the myriad ways you'll change?

You Are Queer Enough

Rev. Lane-Mairead Campbell

It is not about what others think of you,
What their hearts and eyes and minds hold.
It is about your knowing, about your truth.
Fuck the table
No need to be invited to it.
You have all you need,
In the ways you know who you are,
In the discernment you have done,
In the place where you are in this very moment,
In the tools you have employed:
Earth for groundedness,
Air for the thoughts that have condensed and coalesced,
Fire for the passion that brings you to who you are,
Water for the queer love that calls you in and sustains you.
You are queer enough.
You are trans enough.
You are poly enough.
Comparison does not hold a candle,
To the blaze of you, strong in your truth.
When what began as a whisper is now
A fierce roar,
A reality that cannot be denied.
Remember this when you enter a space where it feels
    like you might not be enough: You belong.
You have everything that you need.
You do not need the approval of others.
You are a gift.

You are loved exactly as you are.
Your magic, your alchemy is needed in this moment.
And if people cannot recognize that,
Fuck them.
Find others who can see and understand you,
For your queerness, in its fullness, is a
    gift to those around you.

Blessing When Applying Testosterone Gel For Gender Affirming Care

Lazerus Justice Jameson

Say first

> Today I choose to love myself enough
> > to welcome change.
> Today I choose to reveal more of who I am on
> > the inside on my outside appearance.
> As I use my T gel, may I join with the
> > Trancestors in a celebration of the risk
> > and bravery of my becoming.

When applying gel (can say one line per pump
or can say all together every time)

> I embrace the gift of being transgender.
> > I carry wisdom in my bones.
> I use this Medicine to care for my body daily.
> > I am worth fighting for.
> I am loved. I am not in this fight alone.
> I am whole and I am holy.
> > Knowing this makes me tender and strong.

As I wash my hands

> May this water rinse away the excess fear that does
> > not serve me, and replace it with community.
> May this soap cleanse my day of harm, and may I stand
> > with another today in mutual protection and care.
> May this towel absorb my tears and worry
> > and replace them with the assurance
> > of authenticity and self-love.

As I place my shirt on as a barrier for others to
  not be affected by my gel as it dries

May I use my strength to love more fiercely trans
people and other marginalized people around me
more than I did yesterday. When I need protection
and care, May I have the strength to be vulnerable.

Repeat

Today I have chosen to love myself enough to
welcome change. Today I have chosen to reveal more
of who I am on the inside on my outside appearance.
I join with the Trancestors in a celebration of the
risk and bravery of our collective becoming.

(Amen)

Before Taking a Daily Medication

Bren

O great Peace, thank you for this day. Out of the fruits of the earth and the gifts of reasoning, creativity, and love, we are blessed with just what we need.

As I take this dose, may I be inspired inwardly just as I am transformed outwardly. May I seek the goodness inside of all living things, and see the beauty of the world we can build. For we are called to grow, we are called to synthesize, and we are called to transform.

Amen.

Blessing When Taking Estrogen Pills

Siobhan Reardon

In the morning

I greet the day with a smile. I seek joy.
I am grateful to show the world the true me, for living
    another day better knowing myself. I seek peace.
Though I may be scared, I seek courage.
I take my estrogen for myself and others, so I
    may live a fuller life inside and out, so my
    queer siblings in spirit are not alone.

Throughout the day

I am human. I am trans. I am deserving of dignity.
I am blessed by my transness and I
    embrace my femininity.
The world may be frightening, but I
    stand tall and walk freely.
I set my fear down—that rock that has
    dragged me under far too long.
I take my estrogen because I have chosen
    truth and authenticity.
I know myself better for it, drawing me closer
    to others and the world around me.
I am human. I am trans. I am beloved.

In the evening

I take my estrogen for myself and for others, so
    I may live a fuller life inside and out, so my
    queer siblings in spirit are not alone.
Though I may be scared, I seek courage.
I am grateful to show the world the true me, for living
    another day better knowing myself. I seek peace.
I end the day with another smile. I seek joy.

Wild & Free

Sean Neil-Barron

What must you surrender...
without map, without guarantee,
what holy chaos spills out,
what gorgeous wreckage blooms
when you finally stop pretending you were ever in control?

What drags you back to your bones?
Back to the feral, electric rivers
that knew you before you had a name,
before someone convinced you
that untamed meant broken,
that wild meant wrong.

Look at the barriers we built.
Look how we cage ourselves and each other,
call it safety, call it wisdom,
call it anything but cruelty
...this slow suffocation we perfected,
...this violence we dress up as inevitable control,
...as law
...as love.

Here me when I say this:
we were never trespassers here,
never strangers to life.
Belonged from first breath,
from the first time we screamed
and meant it.

FOR THE
BREAKING POINTS

*When everything feels
too heavy to carry alone*

A Blessing For Trans Federal Employees

Sean Neil-Barron

Here's what they miscalculated: they think you're a line
item they can delete with paperwork, but you've been
practicing resurrection since you learned your own name.

Blessed are you who badge in knowing
they're budgeting your extinction.
Blessed are your steady hands drafting
policy while they policy you to death.

Blessed are your bathroom breaks, your coffee runs, your
thirty-minute lunches, because existing while trans in
federal buildings is now the best sort of tasty treason.

They're defunding your bloodstream and
funding your conversion. Marvel at that
equation. They'll bankroll someone to pray you
straight but not to keep you breathing.

But here's what they forgot: you've been choosing
impossible things your whole damn life. You picked a
name when the world said you didn't deserve one. You
walked through doors marked "authorized personnel only"
just to take a piss. You know the weight of choices that
should never exist, and you carry them like breathing.

Blessed are the non-choices racing toward you like
policy bullets. Stay or scatter. Fight or fold. Mortgage
your hormones or mortgage your future. These aren't
choices—they're hostage situations dressed up as options.

Blessed are you who refuse to negotiate with terrorists,
even when the terrorists wear suits and issue memos.

Blessed are the friends who GoFundMe your
testosterone, the chosen family who forward
job postings at 2 AM, the lovers who hold you
while you do survival math in their kitchen.

They want isolation?
Build community like it's the last thing you'll ever do.
They want desperation?
Share resources like rebellion, the more
you give, the bigger we get.
They want shame?
Love yourself like the middle finger you
are to their small imaginations.

The thing about people who've had to fight for
everything—we don't break clean and we sure as hell
don't break alone. We bend. We adapt. We multiply.

So here's your assignment: outlast the bastards.

When the Dam Breaks, Let it Be Glitter

Jes Martinez-Hunt

When the breaking point comes,
may it arrive without apology.
Bursting through every careful wall
you stacked brick by brick,
to prove you can finally stop guarding the flood.

May the rush be spectacular.
May it sparkle with all the pieces
you no longer need to carry:
the too-small expectations,
the worn-out disguises,
the heavy shoulds you kept out of duty.
Let them all go shimmering downstream.

May the collapse feel like baptism,
an immersion into honesty,
a plunge into the wide river of being.
A holy soaking in your own aliveness.
And when you come up dripping,
may you also shake with laughter.

May you know this breaking
is not the end of you.
It is permission to begin again,
glittering, saturated,
free.

And when the waters settle,
may you find yourself held,
by love itself:
steady, outrageous, unrelenting love,
shimmering forward,
again and again
and again.

For the Times We Are Afraid and Risk Living Anyways

Wendy Bartel

Your heart broken a thousand times
by the confinement of other people's imaginations
trying to box you in, ascribe limits,
tell you the rules, how you 'should be'...
I tell you, your life is a blessing simply for being.

Your gifts of turning the impossible into beauty,
offensive epithets into grace, judgment into freedom
just by your breathing, just by you living as you do;
fabulous and fierce, tender and tenacious, humble, tired
I tell you, you are blessed and a blessing here and now.

Though some have not learned to behold you, that
does not mean you need to shrink for their comfort,
nor be less than you are. It is they who need to grow
to learn how to feel their fear and risk living wildly
enough to grasp the blessing that you truly are.

Responding to Hate

Sean Neil-Barron

Being wildly and unambiguously Trans affirming in
our community means we get transphobic letters.
Who use Christianity as an excuse to hate. We could
ignore them, but honestly? Sometimes they deserve
a response—not to argue, but to name a deeper
truth. This is a response to one such letter.

Dear Letter Writer,

You didn't leave a return address but if
you did, this is what I would say.
There is a love wider than fear, deeper than control,
queerer than we were ever taught to expect. A love that
delights in people becoming more themselves, not
less. A love that whispers to every trans and nonbinary
kid: You are real. You are holy. You are enough.

Even though I am not Christian, I can still answer the
question you pose: What kind of Christian love affirms
trans kids? The kind that actually listens to Jesus. The kind
that knows fear isn't faith. The kind that understands love
was never meant to be a cage—it was meant to set us free.
And here's the truth:
A child discovering who they are is not a tragedy.
A child being safe enough to tell the truth is not a threat.
A child being met with love instead of shame is not abuse.
But denying them that love? That is a tragedy.
That is a threat to their dignity. That is abuse.

So here's my street-corner, megaphone sermon:
Life is vast. Love is vaster. And if your faith has to
erase someone to feel safe, it's not faith—it's fear.

But good news, my dear letter writing friend: There's
a better way. It's big and bright and free. And whether
you believe it or not, you are already held in that love.

May you know it someday. May you let
it in. May you freakin' sparkle.

Blessing for Visibility Chosen, Not Demanded

Sean Neil-Barron

Dear Fierce One,
I don't know your name, but I know your fire—the kind
that burns in queer hearts that refuse to be dimmed.

You could have stayed stealth. Could have kept your
head down, your truth tucked away, your brightness on
low beam. And that would have been completely, utterly
okay. Staying safe isn't cowardice—it's survival, and
survival is sacred. Your right to privacy, to protection, to
choosing when and how you show up in this world—that's
holy ground, and no one gets to tell you otherwise.

But something stubborn and beautiful in you said not
this time—said love means lighting the whole damn
room, even when it makes you a target. Maybe you're
organizing, maybe you're just living loud, maybe you're
the only out queer kid someone else will see today.

So you stepped up. Not because you had to carry the
whole broken world on your shoulders—that's not your
job, never was your job. But because you could shoulder
some of the work. Because you had communities that
held you, and reminded you of your unshakeable worth.
You turned all of that into a weapon of mass liberation.

The bullies came. Of course they did. Bullies always hunt
the brightest flames first. But here's what they missed:
you didn't burn out. You burned through. Straight to

the lawmakers' offices, the school administrators, the places where power lives. You're teaching adults how democracy actually works, one meeting at a time.

You're not just surviving this dystopian moment—you're rewriting it. Not because it's your burden to bear, but because you chose to pick up this particular piece of the work.

This is what sacred looks like today: scared teenagers who know they don't owe the world their visibility but choose it anyway. Queer kids with defiant flames in their chests, carrying what they can, lighting the way forward for all of us.

You are not alone. Behind you burns a constellation of faith communities, chosen families, and stubborn hearts who know that our faith means nothing if we don't fight for each other.

Keep burning, beautiful human. Keep showing us what courage looks like with homework and hope and a future worth building together.

Reminding us that we are fierce, together.

The Gospel According to an Internet Troll: A Found Poem

Katie Watkins

Remember   in my community?

                    pastors
              call abortion "divine"
                              the ones who

Call   abuse   to light

      support   teachers

           do justice

                              paying attention &
      protecting   kids

Remember these sick predators in my community?

((The ones who have drag shows for kids,
sexualize babies, traffic young people here to
be mutilated - whose pastors medicalize other
people's children, call abortion "divine" and
push porn in our schools? You know, the ones who
get money from billionaires and influence our
schools?))

Well it It looks like they also:

Call my child's abuse coming to light "an anti-
Igbq campaign"
wrote support letters to the groomer teachers

the vice principal of the school is deeply
involved with this trans cult church

wife is pushing the church's "Be More Gay, Be
More Trans" campaign in our schools.

Oh, and they call on the congregation to "sleuth
and do justice" to me.

It would be a shame if they went viral and
people actually started paying attention &
protecting the kids in this community from them.

*Note on Source Material:The above excerpt contains inflammatory
rhetoric sourced from a public social media post. It is included
here as found text to be recontextualized into a poetic work. The
views expressed are not endorsed.

Remember

Wendy Bartel

In the quiet moments of doubt,
for the times when you are afraid,
when the world is too MUCH or too little, if
your queer heart
your gender fabulous spirit
has been broken yet again,
remember there is a Love that is holding you
and always will.
Be the blessing you are called to be.

You Are Not Alone

Rev. Jekaren Bell

You are not alone
Though the path ahead
Seems uncertain and cold
Littered with discarded
Promises and fragments
Of dreams
Though the journey
With all its
Twists and turns
Bend in uncomfortable places
Of contention
Though the road
Paved hard
Unforgiving and inflexible
Hold you while you
Aim to root deep
You are not alone

There is no time
Where you will take a step
And not have the shadow of
All that makes you
You are not alone
When the emptiness lingers
A little longer
Each time settling in
It will move
To make space for me
You are not alone

The choices you make
While deceptively yours
Include more than
You
And me
And we are always going to be
In the thick of it together
You are not alone

Let me hold your hand
And brush your hair
As you fight
Fight to rise and
Be free
You are not alone

It's easier if you are
There's no reason to try
To swim against the current
It doesn't want to take you under
It just is what it is
And you
Are who you are
And you are not alone.

FOR THE CELEBRATIONS

*When joy demands witnesses and
pride needs proclamation*

Blessing for Transformation:
On Receiving Gender Affirming Surgery

Rev. Sara Lawall

A spark inside you has been burning
Your inner knowing whispering
Awaiting for the moment when you knew
You

Moving through this life
With more clarity, more joy,
more assuredness in
You

Inviting your beloveds into your inner heart
To accompany You
Support You
Love You
In your quest to be just
You

Until the right time arrived
To cross another threshold in your
Transformation

And now your body
Aligns with your soul
And it sings
More loudly, more brightly,
More expressively
More of You revealed

And we sing with You
Champions of your courage
Blessing the path unfolding before you
With freedom unbound
Marveling at that spark
That divine spark
Sparkling
Shining more brightly in
You

In this time of healing
Cultivate rest
Let your heart lead you
In gratitude for
You
For all You have embraced
And the life that embraces You

For You are
And always have been
The blessing unfolding
Transformed and transforming
Whole and holy
You

For A New Gender Transition

Rev. Lane-Mairead Campbell

Beloved, we are so proud of the new YOU you have
    stitched together. From realizations about
who you are
who you were
who you will become.

Bless the awakening, the reckoning with the truth of you.
May this new and tender, precious peace of you
Be met with kindness
Be met with generosity.
Be met with a love so deep it can honor and hold
    all of you. This newness, this awkwardness
this living into is sacred and beautiful.

It may not always feel that way,
And you may not always be met with the
    acceptance you deserve, but please know
    that you are loved in this becoming
that there is nothing you need to do more
than be who you are now.
The ancestors offer you protection.
The ancestors offer you beauty.
The ancestors offer you their stories

As maps and guidance as you slowly peel away
The protective barrier between the world and what has had
    to remain hidden. If there are losses felt in this time,
may the future hold moments of knowing
that whatever you have lost was not for you.

Who you are now right now in this present
    moment is the truth is enough
is beautiful
even and especially when it doesn't feel so.
May you know the ancestors,
the trancestors

the muthas and the daddies
are all with you
behind you
around you
within you.

May you know the love of a community
here already and still to be forming
to welcome you fully as you are.
May this transition, this forming edge, be blessed
You are a gift.
You are a blessing.
Thank you for sharing who you are.

A Prayer for Be More Gay

Sean Neil-Barron

This is a prayer for more gayness, more
    transness, more queerness.
Because the sum of all of these is being more love.

Spirit of life, Great rainbow of love— The bastards are
at our doors and we could shrink, could play it straight,
could crawl back into closets that never fit us anyway.

But silence has always meant death. So here we stand.
Not silent. Claiming our birthright: Joy.

Queer Joy is coming out for the first time, For the
hundredth time, For the time that finally sticks.

Queer Joy is drag queens voguing at midnight
And reading to kids at 10 AM sharp.

Queer Joy is putting on a binder for the first time
And finding your breath,
Your pronouns at the doctor,
Your true name like it was never a question.

Queer Joy is choosing family
That loves all of you,
Not just the conforming parts.

Queer Joy is kinky and tender,
Leather harnesses and mom jeans,

Doing laundry for a family
You never thought you'd have.

Queer Joy is young voices
Blowing the gender horizon
Into a thousand beautiful pieces.

Queer Joy is kitchen table polyamory
And love that doesn't color inside the lines.

Queer Joy is your whole, full, Unabashed self
In a world that profits from your shame.

This glittery power
Proclaimed on dance floors and at PTA meetings
Terrifies those who need the world
Contained, orderly, and dead.

But Spirit, we know: Love can never be contained,
Never be orderly, And is never, ever done.

We are called to be more love—
Especially now,
Especially when it feels impossible.

Let the people say, amen.

Give Us This Day, Our Daily PrEP

Sean Neil-Barron

Here's what they don't tell you about resurrection—
it comes in amber bottles with child-proof caps,
Costs twenty-four dollars with good insurance
and everything you've got without it.

They're still out here weaponizing God's name
against your medicine cabinet,
calling prevention pride
    as if the divine didn't design bodies
    that hunger for more than bread alone.

But watch this daily miracle:
Someone swallows their rebellion with breakfast.
Someone turns a pill into prayer,
    a prescription into prophecy,
    tomorrow into something you
    can taste on your tongue.

Give us this day our daily PrEP—
    our love letter to everyone we lost,
    our middle finger raised to every plague
    that tried to teach us wanting was dying.

Blessed are the doctors writing hope in medical shorthand.
Blessed are the pharmacists banishing inevitability,
Blessed are you having all the sex— messy,
    holy, unrepentant—
turning flesh into temple,

pleasure into the kind of prayer that
        makes bigots cover their ears
and makes the universe lean in closer,
And smile.

This is what the kin-dom looks like:
PrEP next to your toothbrush,
PEP on everyone's lips,
a future—sharper, sweeter, saltier—
that was never theirs to ration.

We're finally done asking permission to
        swallow tomorrow whole.

Blessing Inspired by a prayer written by Rev. Kelley Colwell

A Blessing for Coming Out in Middle Age

Sean Neil-Barron

This is a blessing for the tender revolution of
finally getting tired of dying politely.

This is for you who spent forty-seven years building
altars to everyone else's comfort, who made yourself
small enough to fit in their frightened prayers, who
learned to genuflect before their tiny, terrified gods.

They sold you silence and called it safety.
They sold you hiding and called it holy. They
built you a closet and called it home.

But blessed are you who finally ran out of room
for their lies, who looked at all those years of
swallowing yourself whole and said: no more.

Blessed are you who discovered that the door was
never locked from the outside, who learned that
coming out in middle age isn't arriving late to your
own life— it's showing up exactly when you're
strong enough to break your own chains.

You were never broken. You were never too
much. You were never supposed to apologize
for refusing to be their comfortable fiction.

This is a blessing for every closet door you crack open, for every truth that spills out like light through prison bars, for every day you choose to breathe like you actually mean it.

The world has been waiting for exactly
who you've always been.

Go knock on every door that needs opening.

A Blessing for Chosen Family (Which Is a Lie)

Sean Neil-Barron

It's a lie: the chosen part (not the blessing).

As if you picked us from a catalog. As if you could
have walked away. As if this were a door you opened
instead of a threshold you fell through, stumbling,
half-dressed, carrying nothing but your breaking.

We don't choose family. Family chooses us.

It assembles itself the way rivers assemble—stitching
and committing, entangling and retangling, wearing
grooves in the landscape of you until there's no telling
where you end and the current begins. Until the
choosing is done for you, for us, until one morning you
wake up with keys to three apartments you don't live
in and someone's kid calls you auntie and you don't
remember agreeing to this but here you are, stuck.

Stuck in the best way. Stuck like roots finding water.
Stuck like the scar that's stronger than what it healed.

Because family that finds you doesn't ask if you're ready. It
arrives with groceries when you're too broken to eat. It sits
in the ER at 3 AM learning the shape of your fear. It knows
your coffee order and your therapist's name and which
ex we don't mention and it knows because it stayed—not
because you chose it but because it chose you back, again
and again, in the smallest ways that build a world.

This is what happens when you stop trying to
construct love and let it construct you instead.

Blessed are the ones who stayed when they could have left.

Blessed are the ones who left and came
back different, better, ready.

Blessed are the midnight calls and the "I'm five minutes
away" texts and the way someone remembers your
birthday when you're trying to forget you were ever born.

May you be chosen. May you choose back.
May the family that finds you be stubborn as
morning, tender as the truth, wild as the actual
shape love makes when no one's watching.

May your family tree grow sideways, backwards,
in loops and spirals—a constellation that refuses
the straight line from root to branch. May it
tangle like galaxies, like mycelium, like the actual
shape of how love moves when you stop forcing
it into charts that only know up and down.

May you be held in a web with tops and bottoms and
verses and switches—a constellation that refuses
hierarchy, that says everyone gets to hold and be held—
until you can't tell who's holding who anymore and it
doesn't matter because you're all holding each other and
that's what keeps the whole damn thing from collapsing.

A Spell for the Stubbornly Bi

Sean Neil-Barron

Listen: your queerness isn't measured by who's in
    your bed tonight. It's not a card they revoke
    when you fall for the "wrong" gender.
You were never straight.
Never a spy.
Never their "see, we told you it was just a phase" trophy.
Never their proof that if you just wait long enough
    everyone comes around to normal.

Cast out the people of all stripes who need you
    to look queer enough to believe you.

Cast out the binary thinking that insists you pick a lane
    like you're merging onto the highway to legitimacy.

Cast out the voice that whispers: maybe they were
    right, maybe you were just confused.

Your life is not parking—it needs no validation.
Not even from the scared part of yourself that
    wonders if you're stealing space.

You contain multitudes,
real, without need to perform or prove.

Here's what they won't tell you:
Your queerness speaks in compound sentences.
Your heart conjugates in futures they
    haven't invented grammar for yet.

You're the living proof that the binary was
    always just bad translation.

The wideness of your love isn't greed, it's grammar.
It knows desire isn't a border crossing,
    it's a both/and benediction.
It craves salt and sweet in the same bite and
calls it dinner,
calls it holy,
calls it exactly what you meant to order.

So speak it.
Punctuate your life with it.
Refuse their filing systems and break their neat little boxes
like the cheap furniture they always were.
You are not half of anything.
You are fluent, whole, and entirely you.
Not straight. Not lost. Still ours.
Always have been. Always will be.
You magnificent both/and creature.
Now go forth and refuse to choose.

FOR THE QUIET MOMENTS

When tenderness is everything

A Blessing Before the Next Shoe Drops

Sean Neil-Barron

Blessed are you who know the world is no "just" place,
that it doesn't get better unless we drag it,
kicking and screaming toward mercy,

The battle never ceases, friend.

Blessed are you who still stop,
and,
watch the light hit your lover's face just right,
who notice the kid on the bus
reading the book that saved your life once,
who know that revolution starts
with refusing to let them kill
the tender parts of you.

The miracle isn't that we're winning,
the miracle is that we're still here,
still choosing each other,
still believing tomorrow deserves us.

Blessing For the Ones Still Figuring It Out

Sean Neil-Barron

Listen: the closet isn't always a cage.
Sometimes it's a cocoon,
a laboratory,
a place where truth ferments in its own sweet time.

The world will tell you hurry up,
pick a lane, choose a label,
as if your heart were Amazon Prime
and truth arrives with free shipping.

Pay them no mind.

Your timeline belongs to you,
not to pride month deadlines,
not to coming-out day countdowns,
not to the well-meaning friends who think
visibility is the only kind of courage.

Some of us are archaeologists of our own hearts,
brushing dirt from buried truths
with the gentleness of someone who knows
that broken things can still be priceless.

You are already perfect in your uncertainty,
already whole in your hiddenness,
already claimed by a love so fierce
it doesn't need a spotlight to burn bright.

The queer ancestors whisper: *We survived the
silence so you could set your own volume.*

Take your time,
Remember, it's all beauty.

three prayers as my spouse clippers my hair

Mx. K Childs

Are you sure you don't want to– they ask

> Hear this, my fervent prayer:
> to be *sure* of anything.
> to discover cause and effect to be exactly as expected.

> *(No, my love, I'm sure I don't want to go to–)*
> To be *sure* that I could walk in -
> salon, barbershop, somewhere, anywhere -
> and even know what I want my face to look like.

> *(Do you remember, my love, when I went to the queer salon?*
> *and even they could not imagine between*
> > *this and that, here and there?)*

> To be sure my request would even be heard.

> *(Yes, my love, i'm sure I want you to cut my hair)*
> Hear this, my fervent prayer.

Bzzzzzzzzzzzzz

Hear this, my groan of gratitude.
Each pass against my scalp, ecstasy.
Liberation,
from only a few inches.
It seems so little,
but it feels like freedom.

Look up, **they say**

I lift my eyes unto–
notice the cobwebs on the ceiling, as they
smooth edges, lines, contours.

Hear this, I am struck speechless at
the everyday wonder.
To be able to love this way.
To be able to live this way.
Their fingertips raising shivers on the shell of
my ear, my scalp, the nape of my neck.
For everyday awe.
Amen, amen.

a lament, as I repack my suitcase (again)

Mx. K Childs

No, not that one
>*shed a tear*

Sequins, too, return to the closet
>*shed a tear*

Too much, too queer
>*shed a tear*

Is this graphic T suspicious?
>*shed a tear*

Travel outfit, set aside (I didn't know you even
>owned a cross necklace, my teenager says)
>*shed a tear*

I disappear amongst a thousand faces
A tear shed into the ocean of travelers
Sparkle may not cross the border, but for
>the ones I love I will let it go
>*shed a tear*

Blessing for Bodies Meeting Briefly

Sean Neil-Barron

As skin finds skin and breath mingles with breath,
As names hang in the air like question marks—

For this brief meeting,
This communion of want,
may you emerge more anchored than adrift,
more found than lost.

Your pleasure, not sin.
Your hunger, not wound.
Your bodies, not battlegrounds but playgrounds.

May you find in the trembling a fierce kind of prayer, in
the touching, proof that you are worthy of being reached
for. That you are holy in your wanting, sacred in your
choosing, blessed in your becoming.

The love that seeks you out doesn't
        always promise forever—
sometimes it shows up naked, laughing, unashamed,
reminding you that some temples you
        only visit once in a lifetime,
that some prayers are answered with salt and
        sweat and the sound of your own name
        called back from the dark like a bell.

Laurentide

HV

I'm from a land built slowly,
Where aching frozen rivers carved themselves
Painstakingly across the soft flesh of the earth into
Gentle hills and deep lakes I called "boring"
In a different phase of my life.

Now that the world threatens to burn down around me,
I'm letting the glacier share its truth
Held in the landscape of evidence:
Something slow and gentle can stop
    my heart with wonder.

And if the glacier took seventy five thousand years
To make some nice hills,
I can take as long as I need to make a revolution
That contains all the appetites of my heart.

With this in mind,
Of course I have time —
Time to draw pleasure out of the soft landscape of her body
With all the urgency of the Pleistocene,
To trace the years on her flesh and see that a lifetime
    is somehow a blip And a whole universe,
To refuse to rush when my heart still races
As her fingertips graze my skin.

Of course I have time —

Time to let our canoe drift with our
        paddles across our laps,
To stage-whisper about the family of turtles

Charging in the midday sun,
To gasp in wonder as we watch one dive into the water,
Visible until she swims down past the sunlight's reach.

Of course I have time for them.
This lake.
This body.
This earth.
These children.
This love.

In them, time concertinas into
Now-Then-Always,
And the easy politics of revolution
Slip through my fingers—
An empty hand is
All the better to touch the love
I am fighting for.

FOR THE FIGHT

When resistance is the only prayer that makes sense

Hope Follows Us

Sam Ames

Listen. We cannot predicate fighting on winning.
We're going to lose a lot in the days to come, and if
we're going to make it through the nights we need to
find something to fuel us that runs deeper than hope.
We're past hope. We don't fight because we think we're
going to win; we fight because it's how we hold on to
what makes us human. That instinct to take care of each
other is the best of us. It's also something we queers
have spent millennia getting very, very good at.

It's easy to forget how recently it is that we've located
victory in the halls of power — our advocates have
secured such significant wins in government these past
years that we've almost forgotten we were forged in loss.
With few exceptions, the most important moments in
our history have almost always been about a handful of
friends trying to protect each other from the uniquely
cruel brand of annihilation scored by laughter. Stonewall,
Compton's, Cooper Donuts. I'm not sure what formal
legal equality would have meant to our ancestors who
used their bodies as shields between lovers and police
batons, or held hands in defiance as officers of the court
burned them at the stake. I do suspect they knew what
we could stand to remember: you can't burn us all.

Even when we lose the battle — and we lose a whole lot more than we win — they have never, not even once, rid the world of us. They can make our lives hell. They can strip us of our rights, our dignity, our future. And if past is prologue, they will. But when they're done, we will still be here. Because our existence isn't predicated on our rights or our dignity or our future. We live not on hope that things get better, but past hope. We live because, in a way not quite replicable in any other community, we are defined by how we love each other. We've spent centuries fighting to keep the people we love alive another night, knowing full well a night will come when we can't.

Part of the legacy we inherit as queer people is that, as soon as we know who we are, we know loss. What those who came before us did in the face of that kind of temporariness was take each borrowed day and distill as much beautiful, heartbreaking, fabulous life from it as possible. We could probably take a lesson or two from those forbears in the difficult days ahead of us. If we only fight because we think we'll win, we aren't going to last as long as we're needed.

Looking around at our country, I don't have a lot
in common with the people winning right now.
I don't want to. I don't think you do either.
Our ancestors weren't winners, they were freaks and
weirdos. I say this with great pride. Queer people are
and have always been losers. And we're really, really
good at it. The truth is, winners are no good in a fight.
Hope is too fragile a muscle. When push comes to
shove, I pick the losers every time. We live past hope.
We fight because we love each other too much to listen
to reason. And we're still here — not because we won,
but because we're part of what it means to be human.

We don't follow hope. Hope follows us.

For Those Who Would Deny Us

Jes Martinez-Hunt

To those who fear us, I wish you a life beyond
fear. May the bars of the cage you built for others
swing wide, and may you discover that the open
air has been waiting for you all along.

To those who call us shameful, I wish you freedom from
your own shame. May you wake one morning and find
that nothing in you needs to be hidden. May you rest in
the relief of meeting yourself fully, without disguise.

To those who try to make us smaller, I wish you the
vastness you've been missing. May you feel what it
is to live without shrinking, to stretch fully into your
own skin, to know yourself as wide as the horizon.

I do not wish you harm. I wish you joy. May you be
undone by tenderness. May you be startled by love. May
you discover what it is to live radiant and unashamed

Tell on Ourselves

Sean Neil-Barron

They want us to snitch on love, so let's snitch on love.

They've built a digital confessional booth where neighbors
can whisper about the kid next door who cut their
hair short, where coworkers can rat out the teacher
who uses different pronouns, where anyone with a
grudge and a WiFi connection can turn caring into a
crime. They call it protecting children. We call it what
it is: a bounty system for breaking families apart.

Tell on us for holding our trans daughter's hand through
high school. For buying our son his first binder and
watching his shoulders drop with relief. For driving
three states over because our kid deserved a doctor
who saw their humanity first. For staying up until 2
AM googling "how to love your queer child better."

Report us for saying "we see you" instead of "we'll fix
you." For believing our children when they tell us who
they are. For teaching that their bodies belong to them.

Tell on the grandmothers learning new pronouns at
75, hearts steady as lighthouses. Tell on the fathers
who threw out old playbooks about boys and girls
and wrote new ones about raising humans.

Here's what they don't get:

Love multiplies when you try to divide it.
Every family they target creates ten more allies.
Every story they silence becomes a song
someone else learns to sing.

They think they're hunting monsters,
but they're chasing ghosts.
They think they are praying for miracles, while missing
that we are living miracles, telling bedtime stories that
end with "you are exactly who you're supposed to be."

So crash their servers with our stories.

Tell on us for loving louder than they can legislate.

Now go love somebody so hard it
breaks their algorithms apart.

For Breaking the Dams

Sean Neil-Barron

Blessed are you who feel the pressure building, behind
the careful walls you've built, behind the stone-stacked
reasons why you cannot, behind the dam of "not
yet" and "too much" and "what will they think?"

Listen, do you hear it? That thunder-rumble
beneath your breastbone, that ancient roar
of waters wanting their true course?

Give yourself over.

**Give yourself over to the terrifying algebra of
aliveness**, to the wild mathematics of what you might
become if you stopped calculating safety, stopped
measuring the flood plain of your dreams.

Yes, you will drown some of who you used to be.
Yes, the valley below will change forever.
Yes, there will be debris
old stories swept away, familiar landmarks
underwater, the careful gardens of your
smaller self claimed by the surge.

This is the courage that calls you: Not the absence
of fear, but the fierce love that says *flowing with
the river matters more than clinging to the banks.*

So crack yourself open like morning.
Split like seed casings in spring rain.
Let the torrent of your emerging self carve
new canyons through your certainty.

Give yourself over to the flood-force of
more life, to the terrible abundance waiting
on the other side of your breaking.

Trust the current.

Trust the ancient knowing that water always
finds its way to where it's meant to flow.

And when the waters settle, when the silt clears,

you will stand in a landscape you never dared to dream—

wider, wilder, and finally free.

Blessed be the breaking.
Blessed be the flow.
Blessed be the courage to let the river go.

Opting In

HV

The Supreme Court says that you can opt your
kid out of knowing that my family exists. That
you can opt your kid out of cognitive dissonance
between reality and belief (lol good luck).

But as a parent, I think a lot more about what we're
opting our kids in to — what we're trying to make
sure is in their lives so that they can learn to love this
world, both as it is and as it could be, the hard way
(the hard way is the only way, I regret to admit).

We're opting in to a church community that loves them
thoroughly but also knows they need help growing. (And
remembering to use walking feet during coffee hour.)

We're opting them in to friends whose parents
have open doors and open hearts.

We're opting them in to a network of queer grown
ups that is so vast and varied and normalized
I'm pretty sure my kids are bored by it.

We're opting them in to a world where
disagreement is not disrespect (but that we've
got to put in the work to make that true).

We're opting them in to love, and knowing that sometimes what love asks will make us feel uncomfortable, out of control, and on the edge. So go ahead, opt your kid out of knowing that my family exists. We'll be over here opting in because that's what my religious beliefs demand.

Parking Lot Mantra

Sean Neil-Barron

*This ritual is for the hard rooms. The ones where you'll be
misgendered, invalidated, or erased. The meetings where
your humanity is up for debate. The spaces where power
is stacked against you and you can't just walk away.*

Before you walk in, stop. Take three breaths.
Assemble your protection, piece by piece.

Feel behind you

Place your hand on the back of your neck or your
shoulder, somewhere you can feel your own support.

Name them out loud. The ones who have your back:

Behind me gathers _____
*(Ancestors who fought for you without knowing your name,
mentors who nurtured you, friends who text you strength,
lovers who delight in your, trancestors, family of all types,
the kid you used to be who refused to disappear)*

Say as many names as you need.
They're real. They're with you.

Feel within you

Place your hand on your heart or your belly,
somewhere you can feel your own truth.

Name what they cannot take from you:

Within me lives _____
(My dignity, my knowing, my love, my queerness, my right to
exist, the truth of who I am, my body's wisdom, my resilience)
Say what feels true today. It doesn't
have to be the same every time.

Feel before you

Place your hands in front of you, palm outs,
toward the door, toward what's coming.

Name your power to choose:

As I enter, I choose _____.
(to remember I can leave, to keep my voice, to honor my own limits,
to notice what I'm feeling, to stay connected to myself, to take up
the space I need, to belong to myself first)
Say what you need to remember you have power.

Weave it together

Touch your chest three times and
say your complete mantra:

Behind me stands _____. *I am not alone.*
Within me lives _____. *Which can never*
      be taken away.
As I enter, I choose _____. *I have power here.*

FOR THE FUTURE

*When we need to conjure what
we're building together*

How to Build a Queer Future with a Beloved

Rev. Lane-Mairead Campbell

First, find the dreams of your lifelong love,
Listen attentively,
Pay close care to how they live their days,
You can hear beyond the words.
Then, create the image-
Their life is the spell
Collect what you can of their hopes and sustaining images,
Let these guide the pattern,
Apply the material to the fabric.
Spend hours and days stitching the images and the words,
Holding the very thread of their dreams in your fingers.
This is a privilege.
They are magnificent.
Consume every romance novel, every sustaining voice,
    every image of their happiness. Share with their
    ancestors how much you hope to love them in this
    lifetime. You will know when the spell is complete,
Though the demons in your brain might tell you
    that it's not enough. Slide the sticks from
    their waters into the sleeve of fabric,
Braid together the yarn.
These dreams will come true through the both of you,
This queer love that fuels futures,

Hold the piece dearly to your heart
And prepare to give it away.

A Blessing for Queer Parents Dragging Kids to Pride

Sean Neil-Barron

Blessed are you loading sunscreen and snacks
like you're packing for war,
because maybe you are.

Pride used to feel like freedom
now more logistical obligation,
but blessed are you who show up anyway,
who teach your children that love comes
in every color we haven't named yet
and twice as many shapes
as our small hearts were built to hold,
that freedom isn't something you find once
and frame on the wall
but something you choose every morning.

Blessed are your kids who don't understand
why anyone would be angry
about glitter and music and people being happy,
who think the drag queens are just
fancy dress-up like Halloween
but better because everyone's invited.

They see two moms holding hands and think "of course,"
They know that sometimes the ones who love you most
aren't the ones who made you.

Blessed are you when your teenager rolls their eyes
and says this is embarrassing,
not knowing they're carrying antibodies now
against shame they haven't even met yet.

Blessed are you who march not for yourselves
but for the kids who will need this someday,
who plant pride flags like seeds in ground
you hope
    will be softer by the time they bloom.

again—I am Loved by This Earth

Rev. Lane-Mairead Campbell

I did not realize that when you handed me
　　a sachet of seeds and flowers
On a July afternoon along the river,
You were handing me a world of possibilities,
A future I did not know I needed.
From the dirt and the sunshine,
The seed and the soil that have sustained you since birth,
A reminder was born that this Earth loves me,
Held in your smile,
Mixed with the salt of the seas my ancestors live near.
You are magic.
Your love is a magic I want to share,
The gifts of the Earth,
This sweet, clean smell,
Do not ever let me forget,
What awakened in me that day.
Stay here and remind me all the time
That I am loved by this Earth,
That I can return to your sweet grounding
　　again and again and again.
I think of you always when I see lavender,
Snap a picture and send it through the airwaves,
To remind you that you too
Are beloved, abundant, more than enough.

A Remembering for When You Feel the Absence of Queer Elders

Sean Neil-Barron

Dear Child,
We know what you're looking for—the gray-haired
dykes who should be teaching you how to change your
oil and break a heart gently. The trans elders who could
tell you which battles are worth the blood and which
ones are just theater for straight people's comfort. The
gay men who should be at Sunday brunch, explaining
how to throw shade without catching a charge, how to
cruise for connection in a world built on isolation.

When you search for us, you're doing archaeology on
a grief that predates your birth—standing in rooms
that should be three generations deep, waiting for
wisdom from people who got deleted from the timeline.
Erased like typos. Like they were the mistake.
That ache for us? Slippery thing. Not just loneliness.
A bone-deep knowing that something was stolen
before you ever got to hold it. A wound that
queers time itself—you're grieving backwards and
inheriting forwards, living in the slipstream between
what was taken and what you're taking back.

But listen up, hun. We're not gone. Not in the
way Empires like to disappear undesirables;

We are the shiver of recognition when you cruise—that electric moment across a crowded bar, that swipe-right certainty at 2 AM, that knowing glance of inevitable failure of every border built to keep us apart.

We are the joy in your magnificent failures—every time you torch a career that demanded your silence, every relationship that chose truth over tolerance, every bridge you burned because the other side wanted you dead anyway.

We are the pulse in your transgression—the filthy words you know as prayer, the truths you find in the dark, the language you forge that's too feral, too alive to ever be pinned down.

We are the fire in your refusal to be understood on their terms. The wild beating heart of your spectacular inability to just: behave.

And don't forget. And some of us? Still here. Plainly, stubbornly alive. Tired as fuck and fierce as tomorrow, doing our best with bodies that carry too much memory. Find us. Learn from us. Let us be human, not monuments. We're messy and contradictory and sometimes dead wrong. That's queer too—permission to fuck up and still be worthy. Grace to fail at grace itself.

Our absence is the wound. Your presence is the stitching.
Your life is our afterlife. Your joy is
our haunting in reverse.
Our tombstones aren't endings—they're coordinates.
Direction to the army of the beautiful dead who loved you
before you had a name for it. So live like every breath is
both mourning and morning. Dance on our graves—we're
underneath, pushing up the flowers, making the bass
drop harder, turning decomposition into composition.

Sincerely,
Queerly and only slightly indecently,

The ones who came before and refuse to leave.

YOUR BLESSINGS

Use these pages to hold the blessings you need to hear.
Write them. Share Them. Release them.

Contributors

Silen Wellington (they/he) is a sculptor of sound, artist of people, storyteller, witch, composer, genderqueer shapeshifter, and lover, among other things. They make art as an act of service, healing, disruption, and magic. Avidly interdisciplinary, they like to combine art mediums such as spoken word, visual art, ritual performance, loud and fiery eye contact, otherworldly and melting trysts, or something else entirely. Check out their work at SilenWellington.com or on Instagram at @silen_creature.

Rev. Lane-Mairead Campbell (they/them/themme) is a queer, community-based witch who embroiders spells, crafts ritual, and writes in Rochester, New York. Their magic is inspired and sustained by the Genesee River, queer love, and a community of hardy and complicated queer people. They can be found on Instagram at @embroideredspells or at their website, www.embroideredspells.com.

Rev. Lazarus "Laz" Justice Jameson (they/them, they/he with other trans folks) trained Unitarian Universalist at Andover Newton Theological School (MDiv 2015) and then caught the Holy Liberating Ghost of intersectional activism and community chaplaincy and found themselves covered in glitter proudly serving those folks no one else would serve (trans folks, sex workers, leather and kink community, polyam folks, neurodiverse people and all the intersections therein) for seven years in St. Louis and now two years as a red-state refugee in Portland, Oregon. Laz was eventually ordained as a minister with the Progressive Christian Alliance.

Siobhan Lúnasa Reardon. From Greensboro, North Carolina, my name is Siobhan and I am an asexual trans woman. I began my trans adventure when I came out to a church friend over coffee in early 2025. I am a member of Unitarian Universalist Church of Greensboro, am a member of their caring ministry, and do recovery work and queer outreach outside of church. I feel magical.

Bren is an active layperson in her midwestern parish. She is honored to contribute to this volume as she finds hope in our modern world.

Sean Neil-Barron (he/him) is a queer minister, born on Treaty 7 Land in Calgary, Alberta, Canada, who currently lives in Fort Collins, Colorado with his husband Charles. Sean is a Unitarian Universalist, a foster parent, a huge nerd, and a shameless believer that no matter what, we're better, fiercer and ultimately destined to be together. Follow his substack and other projects at civicgrace.com

Jes Martinez-Hunt (they/them) is a genderqueer Unitarian Universalist religious professional, librarian, and community weaver living in Central Florida with their spouse, kids, Aussie, and two cats, amongst mountains of craft supplies and books. They co-founded Trans&, where they help stitch together networks of care and courage for trans folks, justice dreamers, and faith-rooted rabble-rousers. Jes believes in sacred mischief, trans joy, and the holy work of reminding us that love is abundant and we are already enough.

Rev. Wendy Bartel (name.not pronouns.please) Weaving rhythm and rhyme, sound and silence, history and hope, Wendy serves the Love that holds us all as a Unitarian Universalist Co-minister, alongside Wendy's Beloved, Lynn. Honoring this sacred Earth upon which we live, Wendy enjoys fair-trade chocolate, gardening, dismantling ableist hetero-patriarchal white supremacy culture, parenting an awesome UU young adult, and caring for a small shy elder dog.

Katie Watkins (she/her) Words from a restless artist wandering with curiosity through the strange weight and wonder of being alive. Katie can be found on Instagram at @notesonearthing or on her website atwww.notesonearthing.com.

Rev. JeKaren Bell (she/her) is a queer ordained UU minister, poet, and artist. Her ministry centers love through creative expression. She draws from the guidance of her ancestors for spiritual care.

Sara LaWall (she/her) is a Unitarian Universalist minister, Mama Dragon, advocate committed to justice, collective liberation and answering the call of Love in Boise, Idaho. You can find her on Instagram at @preachermami or on Tik Tok at @revsarauu.

Mx. K (they/them) is a storyteller and educator from Montréal, Québec, Canada. They love knitting, iced cream, coffee, fantasy fiction, and getting people together to go deep. You can follow them on Instagram at @montreal_melon.

HV is a queer Wisconsinite who loves sapphic romance novels, baking ambitious cakes, and writing liturgy. Her hottest midwestern take is that Lake Michigan is the best Great Lake.

Sam Ames (they/he) is a civil rights lawyer, policy advocate, and writer focusing on LGBTQI+ issues. They are also a proud lifelong Unitarian Universalist. They can be found on Bluesky at @ SamAmes, Medium at @SamAmesEsq, or on their website at www.thresholdstrategies.org.

About Fierce Together

All proceeds raised from GlitterBlessed will
benefit the work of Fierce Together.

**Mutual aid + Queer & Trans Joy + Creative Expression
+ Northern Colorado = Fierce Together**

We're building networks of mutual care, creative
expression, and queer and trans joy in Northern
Colorado. Because when the world tells us we're
too much, too loud, too visible, we lean into each
other and say, *Actually, we're exactly enough.*

Anchored at Foothills Unitarian Church in Fort Collins,
Colorado, Fierce Together works in partnership with many
individuals and organizations to advance our shared
vision of a world where every LGBTQIA+ person can thrive.

Our Work

Fierce Together Fund

This fund provides direct support to LGBTQIA+ performing artists living or performing in Northern Colorado and facing financial hardship—covering essentials like rent, medical bills, transportation, and supplies. Because art is resistance, and artists deserve to eat.

A Drag Christmas Spectacular

Our annual celebration of queer joy, reclaiming the Christmas story and centering queer and trans lived experience through drag, theater, storytelling, and more. Because the holy family was always a chosen family.

True You

A group for gender-expansive, gender-fluid, trans, and non-binary kids 4-12 years old and their parents or caregivers. Parents gather to share stories, support, learning, and joy, while children play, craft, and connect in a safe and affirming environment. Because every family deserves space to breathe, grow, and belong.

—

The revolution doesn't happen in the headlines—it happens at kitchen tables and in church basements, in drag performances and children's playgroups, in the quiet moments when someone realizes they're not the only one.

Learn more and join us at fiercetogether.org